it's going to be okay, i think.

By
Marcus Escher

DEDICATION

For *you*. You've mad me what I am. Who I am. You are the reason I choose to wake up. You are the reason I keep following this path to an unknown destination. Thank you.

INTRODUCTION

The following is a collection of poetry/short-stories/ thoughts/songs I have had since I decided to pursue a degree in English. I graduated from Oakland University in Auburn Hills, MI in December, 2018. I fell in love with writing as a sophomore in High School. I wrote my first "deep" poem and will never forget scraping up the courage to read it in front of the classroom. I didn't look up from the page until I was finished reading, but the look on my peers faces were awe-strucken (good or bad, I'll never know). The rush was something I'll never forget. Writing became a way for me to see the world through a plethora of lenses. The disassociation of image and word is something I find solace in on a daily basis. We've all heard of people "hiding" behing their words on social media, but I don't "hide" behind my words in this book. I LIVE. I live like it's the first and last breath I'll ever take. One thing I want you, the reader, to take away from this book, is whatever you want to ,ake away from it. It's going to be okay, I think.

PART ONE (I):

POETRY

All those friendly people,

Stealing secrets.

All those friendly people,

Sharing a telephone.

Razor sharp words cut

The tongues of hollowed bones.

Teeth like silk softly brush

The pooling water where

Evil lies.

Oblivious to the rising tide,

What was once so hard & pure

Is now the Sargasso Sea.

Blood-stained; rotten; dead.

All those friendly people,

Sharing secrets.

All those friendly people,

Stealing telephones.

Do not let anyone tell you ghosts are not real.

To some, that is what you are—

just another petal on a "wet black bough."

Sleep, little bird.

You don't have to sing anymore.

Keep your wings closed

& let your heart soar.

Sleep, little bird,

like a stone.

Close your sunken eyes!

You are not far from home.

Illness creeps,

Unnoticed.

Unheard.

It is the bird and you are the worm.

It will hear you scream.

It will watch you squirm.

But, it will always be the bird,

And you will always be the worm.

I hope it does not find me.

Lying in the catacomb of civilization,

smoke swallows the tattered wings

of butterflies that were once beautiful.

A blizzard of ash whips in the violent

Winds.

Hoarse throats & fists clenched!

A pool of tears slides to blood,

as dried muds start the flood.

A sharp tooth penetrates

the soft foot of a newborn child

in the catacomb of civilization.

Vivid memories sleep on the horizon.

Reminiscing on days past,

but not gone.

Asleepbut notdead

negative energy radiates.

Cuts deep-to-the-core totheheart

Hatred | insecurity-depression

DROWN (NOW DR)

Try to swim.

Can't move.

For what worth is this life alone?

Says the insecure

& the one with hate.

Says the one wearing a smoke-colored-lens

The hand has been there.

Hold it!

hearts can be forever stitched

light can captivate your soul

be healed

be free

BE

LEAVE.

Temple built on foundation of lies.

Shack rests on pebbles of truth.

Pig eats mud where I became.

Dove spreads wings in burning flames.

Brain waves shutter a weeping soul.

Lungs ooze tar through open holes.

Wiz-Naw-Sawl said,

"Here I stand

In the fountain of youth.

Where I have

Lived and loved and hated, too.

I-don't-know-how-to-say-it

But it is all a lie."

Wind blow Rain fall Sun hot Snow ball

Temple temple crumble down

We all died with out a sound

Lord God Dad above you are love

& that's enough.

crushed coca cola cans

sprawled out adjacent to

a beaten box of cheerios

spilling its guts to the

neighborhood homeless

woman, Mary.

She claims

she is pregnant but everyone

knows she is overweight—

'cause crushed coca cola cans

& cheerios spilt in the alley.

The darkest clouds will follow you into the light, if you let them.

depressive episodes

    steeped in abusive relationships

brews the worst habit.

one crevice in the dam

    turns to a crack

that becomes a gaping hole.

once the flood

    finds its pace

it will always win.

Dilapidated minds

Engulfed in smoke

& muddy mirrors.

Wrought bones choked

By torn ligaments.

Bruised apples of beaten

Eyes and Is-n-yous-n-alls.

Abolition transformed to society like liquid.

Children still scream & choirs still sing

The vultures still swarm & cows will always moo.

Rib to life life to dirt or ash or mold,

It does not much matter.

Do you ever feel your throat

Well up so tightly

That you can't breathe?

Do you ever wonder

If the one you love

Will one day leave?

Do you ever dance

In the middle of the night?

When the stars are shining

And no one else can see you.

Just last week I had a dream.

I can't fully remember what it entailed.

There was a Cat,

music playing,

and a poplar tree.

I smiled a terrific smile!

My mother said she was proud of me.

She said it was a terrific smile!

I remember a flash came from a camera;

My dad was filming me and the Cat?

The sun broke through the fractured clouds.

My skin was warm.

Only where the sunlight touched, though.

"You really have a terrific smile."

Tuxedo, Wedding dress.

I can't remember everything.

I really do enjoy dreams.

Dreaming of success

In succession of sins.

Taunting filthy habits

Will not let one win.

Crystal clear minds,

& kaleidoscopic eyes.

An aura of progression—

Is the final prize.

Speaking tainted substance,

Or, steadfast grip of the rope.

Takes away the pleasure,

Leaves an empty envelope.

An I within an eye

A mind being mined

Transcendence of the spirit

Is what one hopes to find.

Time has no correlation

To the treasure buried nigh

Time is a selfish bastard

That will go on when one dies.

Absolve of wretched actions

Wash away the tears,

One can live forever

In ever-after years.

I!

a c t

ually (probaly

NO! t) wanting wanted

to be want (wont?) w

ith the (day-in-night-is-

dead—routines that

WILL!!! chew me

and spit me out? into

(1) One. Mill E Yun

different DIE)rections.

You are a fighter.

I am a match

and you are a lighter.

You have made it thus far,

plus, you have made

many lives brighter.

Thank you,

for staying head strong.

Keeping in tune

And singing life's song. (whatever
the hell it is).

Before you know it,

You will be gone.

So,

enjoy the little things,

They do not last long.

Whichever one you choose does not quite matter. However, the way you choose to handle it is precisely what matters.

I'm talking about the fork in the road.
I'm talking about your journey.

So, go ahead, put a blindfold over your eyes and make your move; for you cannot see the end, but you *must* choose.

Just remember, dear anonymous soul, down that road you will travel, so, take it slow and follow it whole.

Life is but a constant circus—a freak show.

City to city state to state all the same.

We are all of the same species, you know?

So we all experience pleasures and shame.

Yet, we continue to run, and can't let go

Of mistakes we've made. We carry the blame.

The ringmaster says, "next stop Heaven or Hell?"

That is my last stop; so, where shall I dwell?

Smush Brain

Nose powdered in cocaine.

It's all a game it's such a shame.

Too late cupcake stood me up on two dates.

It's such a shame it's just a game.

Liquid hands shredded pants

Elephant jump and shout monkey!!

Tap dance!

It's all a game a stupid game.

Open book fingers laced brain heart

different place tears of blood

roll down face.

It's all a game it's such a shame.

god never died but Jesus did&

he is GOD but god has

no form (shapebody) because

He is spirit which is everything

that death takes

away from life. so God does

not die it/he/she/there/where

shifts-shape in-

To another form in dark&light.

There's an infinite amount of energy

but that's not true, right?

Wisdom does not seek age,

Nor does maturity.

For the most grown

May be the most childish.

The most matured, physically,

But the least matured, cognitively.

One must think before one speaks.

Understand the surroundings.

Respect the given situation.

Adapt in a manner in which forgiveness is present.

Strive to be better.

Flourish in peace.

Live in happiness.

Wisdom does not seek age.

I am a shelf.

Holding too many unread books,

Dusty records, and unlit candles.

They walk by me and throw their

Unwants on me. I can support quite

A bit.

Sometimes, I want them to light the wick

And spin the disc. Turn the page & flail their

Arms.

MOSTOFTHETiME!

I want them to just take a second and thank

Me for holding

The weight of their unwanted things 'cause

I'm ready to snap.

I can feel the heat of their skin against me but

It's just a sweaty palm acting as a kickstand so

They don't fall because they know I can support

Them.

The sun-dipped moon

Dripped a golden hue.

The air smelled of honey

The day I married you.

i bent the world
so youcouldcome over
to the other side,

                but you just stared
                and angled your arm

i shouted at the top
of my lungs that you
were a lunatic

                but you just whispered
                and blew your littlenose

i cried for ten days
because it felt appropriate
for your behavior

                but you just laughed
                and walked away

i bent the world
for you so-i-thought
but honestly

                the world bent me for you
                and i *broke.*

i don't know,
i guess.
i keep trying
to grab ahold of it,
but it keeps slipping
through the cracks—
like a handful of sand.

"HAVE YOU TRIED HOLDING IT DIFFERENTLY?"

i am not sure
there is a correct way
to hold it.
i don't know,
        i guess.

I hate myself.

You're incredible.

(I don't believe you).

You're incredible.

(There's no way).

You're incredible.

(You're a liar).

You're incredible.

(Stop lying).

You're incredible.

(I think i believe you).

You're incredible.

(I believe you).

You're incredible.

(I'm incredible).

You're incredible.

(I love myself).

I smoked a wet cigarette

    that cursed my tinted breath

[I] inhaled it 'til my lungs turned black.

    [i] sipped a crystal broken glass &

cracked one of my broken teeth or is it tooth?

when I opened up the book the loose-leaf was reading

                ME!

drop the needle | flip the disc | life does not get any better

than this or does it?

hungry soul walks on tired toes and tries to satiate the

insatiable.

    & fables & folklores & fairy-tales are not real so don't

reel me in.

With a suit and tie and a nice dress.

Take it for what it is, not for granted.

Let's make a pact, Shall we?

To accept the opposition—

Finally make ends convene.

It was you "Pig-Headed Father" who

Immersed my mind with a new wave of thought; But,

It is you, "Devil-Headed Father" whom I intend to make a Pact
with.

Let's leave lust 'lone

But still admire it's beauty, it's frightening glor-if-ication of what
could be.

For you have left me in a trance with your manifest-oh's
As in you are manifesting something with infinite potential and
then—Oh!

Why have you chosen this end? Why have you seemingly turned
your back on all

That is beautiful?

But what

Is

Beauty? It is in the e(I)e of the beholder.

And what you think is beautiful is treacherous to me. Yet,

am awe-stricken by your precise language, your ability to

shape-shift, and to make me second-guess myself. despite us never co-existing.

So, here is to you, to me, and to anyone else who is willing

To handcuff themselves to this precise offer.

Let us, humanity, breathe

Deeply, let us put or consciousness to the way side.

Let us turn the knob quickly to the left on our conscience.

But don't stop there! Break the knob! Just li(v)e,

Li[v]e, live, as if it's the only thing you can do.

I walked a tight rope to the moon.

A drunken sailor sang a tune.

I walked a tight rope to the moon.

A brain-dead bat went weeping, blue.

I walked a tight rope to the moon.

A stop-sign struck a moving car.

Him & her are bizzare!

A stop-sign struck a moving car?

I was baptized in a kitchen sink

With dirty dishes and a Brillo pad.

Second-hand smoke tainted my lungs

Like the peeling wallpaper in the dining room.

The faucet's water rushed over the wrinkles

In my forehead while the crucifix tried to jump

Off the wall.

My father waved his arms angrily and my mother

Wept as the pastor shouted over the radio.

I wasn't cognizant at this point in time,

But I remember how furious he—my father—was

When he dropped his newly lit cigarette on his plaid

Blazer. He was over-the-moon-MAD.

Once, my mom took me to church and this nice couple

Handed her the offering plate. Her hands were shaking,

Violently. She reached in to her purse and the change inside

Was rattling. She pulled out 10 pennies. One for each

commandment?

And she picked me up and ran out crying. She's been an atheist

ever

Since that moment. I don't know if it was the pressure of the

situation

Or what it was, really.

The maniacal laughter of family get-togethers will always rest in

the

Hall I was conceived in.

The blood-stained carpet and broken chandelier will always be who I am.

It isn't a bad thing. I never did get upset about it. It is what it is. I looked that hall in the face with many different faces. From youth to adolescence

To this to that. It's all contained there.

In that hall that's given too many echoes and never said thank you.

I'm falling down this hole

Faster than the rabbit.

See, I'm on a sinking ship and I am the captain.

If I was to die today,

Or tomorrow,

I hope that you know,

I loved you with every fiber.

If I was to die today,

Or the next,

I wish with all my heart,

That this is not the end,

But the start.

If I was to die today,

Or next week,

I want you to know

You mean everything to me.

I died today,

But, before I left

I swear I heard you say:

Don't worry dear,

I booked your flight to Heaven,

Late last night.

It's a one way.

I have mine too!

Tucked away,

In my favorite shoes.

You think just maybe

For tonight,

You can make a pit stop

On the top of the moon?

I'd really love to see you.

I know I'll see you soon."

If you were the dividend

And I was the quotient

Who was the divider

That left us broken?

Immediately lost

Like a dream you

Just awoke from.

That's what it feels

Like to be in an un-

Healthy relationship.

Quilted blankets fold
Like pizza on a warm
July day.

Spaghetti noodles unravel
On to napkins tainted
red, white, and blue.

Spasms of color riddle
The night sky & loud
Bursts make children cry.

Poor Uncle Sam has an
Epileptic episode
& his body convulses.

Chattering teeth and a
Bloody tongue. dirty air
In rotten lungs.

Independence,
Spangled stars,
And song is sung

All before the day is done.

Binging.
Purging.

Nothing feels right.

Those two are not working.

A repetitive cycle of guilt and shame.

Once it starts, nothing is the same.

But, once it ends, everything will change.

The sun will warm your bones.

Those thoughts will leave you 'lone.

And maybe you will finally feel at home.

In your precious skin.

You just have to love yourself—from within.

Is it a death?

It feels like it.

I didn't see anything.

I didn't hear anything.

Six weeks of excitement,

Fear, hope, etcetera.

Diminished.

Now,

It all feels like a dream

That turned out to be

A nightmare.

In time, it will turn back

Into a dream,

But more importantly a

Story of solace.

The mind's eye (mine)

Watched a life that was never

Lived.

The human—my—heart

Felt the strongest love for

Another that it had never met.

Days move in a cyclical motion.

Nights drape a happy notion.

We never thought a bird

Could sing without a word.

Turn the music up-

Side down.

Let the rhythm take

The sound.

At once,

It all happened at the same time.

I knew that he/she was meant

To "die."

It happens for a reason in the coldest

darkest season.

An old friend is someone you don't know

anymore.

If Cindarella can slip on a shoe
Then why is there a cheetah at the zoo?

Bask in knowing that the who and what

Was once a living breathing laughing

Child will never live and never die

Because god in the sky said it's not

The time for a life to learn the hard-

Ships that sail the rocky waves

That will snap the mast & drop the jib

Into oblivion because consciousness

Was never an option, and I am now

Aware and know that no one or nothing

Can give or take away what happens in my

Narrow world protected by a skull that

Will lie in the dirt of many tomorrows

Or be tossed into the unknown that some

Know, but I never will and neither will he/she

So just let it be like the beatles that are crushed

By boots of combat in the desert heat.

Life is sweet but dreams are sweeter.

And I dreamt of you & probably always will.

It's going to be fine, I promise.

It doesn't seem like it, right now.

However, it will get better.

Sometimes, it might go on for weeks.

I knew a kid that didn't feel right again for 10 years, I think.

I don't know, it will all be okay, trust me.

Honestly, you might never feel *completely* normal again.

Being normal is a funny thing, really.

To some people, it's normal to wear two different colored socks.

That's a really bad example, though.

I think you get the point of what I am trying to say, maybe.

Listen, I really think everything is going to work itself out here.

It's not like it was your fault, right?

There's no way that you were the cause of this, you know?

You have always seemed so up beat and positive, to me.

You forgot to wear pants to church when you were 4,

remember?

Actually, that wasn't you, but it was funny.

It might have been a dream I had once, actually.

Look, all I am trying to say is, I *think* everything is going to

work out.

You'll look back at this and smile, probably.

I *can't* promise it's going to be fine.

It's tilted,
hold on.
This might feel a little
Uncomfortable.
It's nothing uncommon.

There's something funny
About the EDGES!

The silent heartbeat was
A black hole with
Funny edges that made me cry.

The black hole was filled with
Love, LAUGHS, and so many
Moments that never happened.

Crystallized eyes disguised
By a head tilted to the floor.
There's something funny
About the edges.

She didn't have to say much more.

kissing clouds &

truly living—for the first time.

steel blue eyes that steal my heart,

holding hands fingers loosely laced.

racing minds with thoughts

that won't stay in place.

all our wrongs we can't erase,

but I never will because

it led to this happy place—you.

finger tips & racing hearts.

body of a goddess I kiss her breasts

she kisses my chest we both caress

and feel—feel every piece of eachother—

she looks me in the eyes before I go inside

and for the first time I know I can hide anywhere

with her beside me.

she digs her nails my heart prevails I don't believe

in fairy tales.

no, this is a dream, a dream I never want to end.

finally no one is holding the pen, no one is turning

the page, this is every day.

here's to you, here's to me, here's to everything we can be,

here's to me falling in to the abyss and knowing I'm falling

into bliss everytime I hear you laugh, I see your smile, and

feel your kiss.

Let us take

A leap of faith

Into parts unknown—

A better place.

Where the past

Can be erased,

And broken dreams

Can be replaced.

By stalwart angels

Saving grace.

They'll speak of love

Face-to-face.

And the One & Only,

The Judge of all,

Will close His case.

Close the door, please.
It's cold as hell &
I am sweating.

How.

I don't know.
Just swing the thing shut.
I'm SHIVERING &
It's burning hot in here.

What.

The door.
Just tap it a little.
I don't know, just
Be gentle with it, please.

Why.

Because,
If you break my door
Then everyone is going
To see what's in my bedroom.

Who.

Everyone!
Dammit, just swing the door shut.
Just kick it with the heaviest
Part of your heel.
Spit on it!

Where.

In the middle, probably.
Maybe the top right &
Lower left hand side.
Honestly, who knows.

When.

Tomorrow. Actually,
I'm not sure I'm up for it.

One day these pages will burn. Like my body, inside an urn.

Paperweight dreams lie on a heavy mattress.

The tides rip the shore and swallows pebbles.

Rose petals melt to newborn babies feet, comfortably.

Antlers move like a nervous dancer—stiff but wild.

Teeth stick to gums and gum gets stuck on shoes.

SO!!!

Better keep the trap shut or a fly might make a home

In the spider's web of tangled words that weave together

In a sensible manner.

When the hooves clap the ground like hands in an empty arena

Everything will probably be okay, but that's not my decision.

Eyes are so peculiar in the way they tell a story.

Some awful. Some not.

Pasted on the frosted glass are palms

of children.

The camera lens absorbs the moment

without saying a word. It holds on to it

& shows what happened exactly as it happened,

but it's different every time.

Life & Death interposed by Time.

All Kin.

Birdies plashed the bath water

Like a mother dips the ankles

of her baby boy to cleanse his skin.

A brain congealed as if it was once

a bowl of soup.

The rendezvous will never see through

because there is no continuity between

the two.

Etched in stone the people sighed there was

a different story in each and every eye.

Let's fly away all alone.

I love your body & fragile bones.

Touch me, kiss me, make me moan.

Hold me tight,

combine our souls.

I'll fly you anywhere, all alone.

Hi
  High
    Up Above
Down Below
  Let's fly away all alone.
You & Me = Ecstasy

In the sky we Rest in Peace.

In & Out.

In & Out.

We breathe alone, scared, but free.

You said it & I reacted

poorly.

Three syllables that change

everything.

The wind still brushes the nape

Of my neck.

The sun still rises & sets & watches

The earth—us—waltz around it.

Everything is different now.

At first,

I was unsure how to feel what to think

Who to tell who to thank.

I mean I really didn't have a good reaction,

And nothing in the universe has really changed.

Stores still open & close & the trash (waste) men

Still run their routes.

Even if I did have a good reaction and I said, "isn't that swell"

Everything would still happen as it always does.

However, when you said it, and you know exactly what you said.

There was a microscopic shift in this strange world we live in.

There was a major shift in our lives, though.

I really wish I would have had a better reaction because

I am excited. Truly.

I want you to be the one who calms my hands when I can't keep them from shaking.

something
>>>IS>>>>>>not
Right & I & You & do NOT

know what IT is.
>>>THEY DID WHAT!?
day whatever and what and we
are still here.
Where is here? (You-might-no-
never-mind).
She cracked that cocunut like a spine
>>>>>>>>>to get to the MILK inside.
run around a circle and tie it like a square.
Shot gun-shells fly out like confetti.

CLAP CALP C!AP
>>>>>>the crowd goes mad. (please/
She said—reading in prose—but it quickly
>>>turned to verse.
Whying and whereing and whoing not howing.
>>>>>>>>>KNOW1
wants to see the foundation of the house. as long
as it is (& it is
PRETTY>>>>>that>>>is>>>>>all they them want to know.
B>>>K M>>>D
>>R A>>>>>E>>>>>O
>>E>>>>>>>>>>>>>W
>>>>>>>>>>>>>>>>N
!!!

I cannot stop you from taking my life;

For you are an unstoppable being.

I beg you do not use a gun or knife.

Please, take me in a way that is freeing.

I've tried to diminish your wicked ways.

Health, Wealth, and Brawn, cannot rid of your cruel,

Demented trickery. How many days,

How many times have you made man the fool?

I know you are out there creeping—haunting

Innocent souls, far too young to feel you.

The way you wrap your fingers is daunting.

To see Him, it is you I must go through.

Tick tock goes the clock on the block I stay,

Father Time haunts me all night, every day.

Application of "beautiful" facades

Cleansing the wretched abuse, with items

That humanity has received from God?

Blocking beauty residing inside 'em.

Just a trace around the lids of the eyes

To eradicate prior perceptions—

People postulated. now go! Disguise!

Put the lines in different directions

To keep the apparitions questioning

How a figure, beautifully striking,

Melancholy in nature, reflecting

The wicked words, where she once wept weary—

Do you understand the message clearly?

O, in time my words will presume me false;

My pages will be another capsule—

For you will rage about them and convulse,

The beauty

Violent vagrants vindicate views

I Do Not Enjoy This Much.

Writing sonnets is a pain in the ass

It doesn't make sense to limit myself

I'd rather smoke crack, or sip on some gas,

Then write a sonnet that won't leave the shelf.

I'm done with rules and regulations; you see,

They keep me grounded in awful places,

It's like being trapped inside a city,

and you'll never get to see new faces.

Hindered by those damned rules, of dumb sonnets

Gives me a peculiar feeling, as

if I am getting sick—I might vomit

I really need to see what the world has—

Yet, I am still marching to the same tune

I am too comfortable to leave soon.

For skies of red and seas of blue converse.

The laughing vagrant taps his thumb (fiercely)

As the white boy carries the broken black hearse

Into the backyard with his family.

A rising sun gives birth to a new day

That passes away into the moon's arms.

The cycle will not cease for those who play.

It is beautiful to live inside harm.

Please do not fear the man above you for

He was once a lost soul drifting without

A clue where to go or who's keeping score

But he stayed true to the path his narrow

small route.

Suzy lost her nickel
At the park last Sunday.

Tommy lost his watch
At the diner today.

Johnny lost his mind
At Church in February.

Billy forgot to laugh
At a joke yesterday.

Mindy made a man
Manic on Monday.

The days will get the best
Of us, too, one day.

The bird was a folly
In the midst of intelligence
That retracted when the wind blew
In the heart of spring.

Wilting flowers withered away
With innocent laughs
That haunt lily pads
Where youth once lived.

The bird was a folly
But it sang, anyway.

I will throw my troubles into the chasm;

Run through meadows, where weeping willows do not weep.

Her and I will make love until orgasm,

And my heart will beat for me to take the leap

Into the great unknown—my eyes-lids will spasm.

A reminder that I must sow what I reap

Or I will find myself diving back into

The chasm, and find that my troubles there grew.

The day you lost your mind,

I lost mine, too.

Your swollen, shaking hands,

In that desolate hospital room.

Haunt me every day;

Leave me feeling blue.

I'm sorry I left your side.

I didn't know what to do.

The owl's eye grabbed me

& I was paralyzed, physically.

I bowed my head slightly forward

& it cracked my brain open like an egg

with it's stone beak.

Unthoughten thoughts permeated

The dirt like poisonous fumes.

Bloody tears seeped

Into the fibers of my shirt—ink

In skin. Scabbed then healed.

The owl's eye controlled me in the night,

But let me free in the light.

You have not always, in the literal sense, stood by my side

Albeit you never strayed too far away.

I used to pick you up in the midst of nights riddled with

depression.

As soon as you stepped in I felt an unequivocal calm overtake

me.

As soon as you touched my lips, I could feel sensations erupting

inside me.

You have offered help—an escape—to a plethora of people

You do not judge upon extremities,

Nor do you give a damn of spiritual standpoints

You simply listen, and help, without saying a word.

For that I thank you.

Yet, I have heard of your wicked demise, as well

You kept my younger brother, Jeremy, company often

I advised him that he ought to slow it down a bit,

But you won him over.

He enjoyed your constant company, and often informed me that

you were the only one who agreed with him, and listened to

every last word that came from his mouth.

But as the years rolled on you betrayed him.

Infested him with an infectious cancer,

Which metastasized, and brought him to his final resting place.

This proved to me that you are filled to the brim with trickery.

I am writing to tell you I have figured out, fortunately, your

cruel deceptions.

I will not succumb to your ways.

I will not let you strip me of my days.

Hello, sir. Hello, ma'am.

I'm in the search for a nice suit. It must,

Be comfortable.

Because I am going to be wearing it for an in-

Definite amount of time.

Do not worry about the price, I'm quite certain

I will be able to foot the bill.

Please, do not

Take me as a finicky individual,

For I'm just incredibly anxious to arrive to the big show.

It's the biggest of all! People,

Argue about when it started to this day,

And there is no true end date; so, PLEASE

Just make sure it is the most fashionable, the most exquisite,

Finely tailored of them all.

"Fits perfectly" H(Sh)e said.

The next I knew I was at the show, still am, with no god-

Damn clue how I got here.

Fiction is an expedition into an uncomfortable place.

It is! malleable.

It is!! kind.

It is anything you want it to be.

It! has! no boundaries!

Up up up up away

Billy Balloon

Up up up up away

Billy Balloon

Billy Balloon a fairy-tale's delight

Drifted off in climax of night.

A Balloon In hand a peace of this man.

When he sails skies skies sail him.

This is a cry this is his cry to save humanity from awful times!

Luna wept: "Billy Balloon don't leave too soon

A hyphen –tic I will adopt and haunt lonely souls in empty rooms."

Gravity yanked his leg but his balloon was a magnet to the moon.

Who can save us? Billy Balloon.

Billy Balloon watches over on his house which seems to loom.

Billy Balloon can make-n-break a man

What is a balloon? A balloon is freedom.

Billy Balloon up up away.

Night after night day after day

Up up up up away.

We're all on the same planet, but we're all in different worlds.

When a tear falls

Like a spider dangling

From its woven web and

Time freezes over

In an instant,

Nothing will be the same

Nor should it.

When I was nineteen (19) I remember making a BOLD statement
to someone.

I was ravenous with artistic rage & wont to create beauty—make
a dent in a world
That has been in too many car accidents. (probably won't find
the dent if I make it).

I said, "THERE ARE PRECISELY TWO (2) WAYS ONE CAN LOOK
AT LIFE."

1. You are born at the bottom of a staircase. You cannot see the
end of the stairs because there are so many. You want to know
what is at the top of the stairs so you start climbing. After a
while, you realize you do not need to take every step, so you
start skipping one, two, three—here and there. Sometimes, your
legs get tired so you sit down and take a break. (nothing wrong
with that). BUT you know you will get up again and keep moving
forward, because who knows what is up there? You already
know what has happened on the other steps so there is no
reason to revisit them. It will take your whole life to get to the
top and the amount of stairs in the staircase is different for
everyone so do not go feeling sorry for yourself. At the top of
the stairs you will be greeted by death. It is okay! At some point
throughout your journey you realized that was your inevitable
demise and became comfortable (maybe even excited) with this.
Everyone has a different greeting when their staircase runs out

and that is what is so great about it. SOME people think that death will greet you with another staircase that never runs out, but no one will ever know until they get to that point and once you get to that point you cannot tell anyone because even the idea of revisiting a step once visited has vanished. If you look at life this way, you know-and-believe that you have done the most that you can do and your life will be fulfilled because you sought out the end. Even when you got tired and your legs hurt and you got nervous about how far you had gotten.

2. You are born at the top of the staircase and life is looking at you with an odd face. You look back for a split-second and before you know it, life pushes you and you are never able to get your bearings because you are falling until you are so beaten, bruised, and shaken up that you hit the ground and die. This is the worst way because from the start you were a victim and everything happened to you. You did not happen to it.

I said this. I do not know if it is true or not but I like to think these are two (2) of the many ways to look at life.

wintry fac-

es faced

)north

in-to

morrows

waste)land.

(9) nine.

rising suns hush

ed

the moon to

black.

some days i feel like

a background actor

in some

one else's play.

That rabid beast stood

Parallel to me.

Its eyes filled—

A map of intersecting

Streets smothered in blood.

Its harrowing shouts

Pierced my ears.

Ready to plunge,

Tear me to shreds

At its leisure—I was

Frozen—waiting to feel

The onslaught of pain

It received pleasure from.

Its tongue—wet and heavy—

Protruded over the slight bump

Of its lip, and dangled

Above its cleft chin.

Saliva trickled down the tongue's edges

Like blood on a jagged knife.

I was its prey.

I was the victim to a cold-hearted

Predator.

I floated in and out

Of consciousness waiting

For an ethereal spirit to save me

From this beast—no luck.

I conformed to its every move.

The nails were sharp, and the movements

Were rapid.

The words it spoke

I could not discern

For I had not imagined such a monster

As the one that tore me to pieces that day

Could exist in a place as peaceful as this.

I have scars all over my body, inside and out,

Yet the common person cannot see them.

I have been told many-a-times it was just a dream

A bad dream—a nightmare. It is simply not possible

For no one can discern that it truly occurred

Due to the inability to visually depict the scars littered

Across my body and riddled throughout my heart.

That wicked, selfish monster did what it pleased.

It left satisfied and full for the day.

I have not seen it since, nor do I hope to again.

If I had not of traveled in those woods alone,

Maybe, just maybe, it would not have tainted me,

Leaving me to a sea of impossible explanation.

God works in mysterious ways.

you find out a lot about life through reactions—chemical, emotional, physical, etc.

For Christ's sake.

Do not put *too* much make up on.

Then it just becomes overbearing,

And takes away from the underlying,

Natural beauty.

Please make sure you use the *exact*

Shade. Present an image to your viewer

He or she will immediately attend to.

Just make sure you don't present a muck

Of hues.

If you so choose to use eye-liner,

Please, make certain of your strokes.

It's a very important matter.

Stay inside the lines.

This is elementary stuff, really.

Now, it is vital the outfit lines up

With all of this excess you've added.

Keep it simple, for God's sake.

Keep it simple.

Don't go wearing a wedding dress

With sandals.

Most of all, though.

It's good to remain formal.

No matter the occasion.

Do *not* let the pressure break

You.

However, if you can *truly* convey the message, then by all means

Let hell break loose.

     Walk completely naked.

You *must* see through a rose-colored lens

    If

    You want to live a fallacy.

You *must* uncover your eyes of any material

        If

        You want to see the world

    For exactly what it is.

You have sat alone

In an empty room,

And pondered death.

It is a natural thing.

You have surfed the internet in hopes

To find someone or something you can

Fall in love with. Even if it is for the night

You can at least be in-love momentarily.

You have laughed,

you have cried,

you have done a lot

Of stupid shit you wish you could take back—you can't.

Through it all, though, you still wake up each morning. Maybe,

You go to work, or send the kids off to school, or wait for the guard

To open the gate. Either way, you are awake.

You have seen some awful things.

Haven't you? Remember when you witnessed

That horrid thing, but did not make a peep.

Or, remember that one time you were all alone

And questioned everything? Then you went outside—

Everyone, even the kids, were staring at you

Because deep down you were scared they knew

Your "dirty little secret."

You have lost

A friend, father, lover, etc.

It does not matter what

It is exactly.

You have lost *something*.

You have won.

That 10k you trained for, for months.

And that softball tournament when you were ten.

Or, what about that trial when you won

Full custody of your child, because there was no way

You would let your kid be with him alone.

It does not matter what

It is exactly

You have won *something*.

Wake up!

You are still here, right?

You are still breathing, right?

Good.

You have the chance to save a life

Today.

You have the chance to make anew.

You are lucky, really.

You have the chance to

Live.

Tomorrow you could

Die.

You have come a long way.

You have a lot farther to go, though.

Just thought I would let you know.

Be a benefactor in an individuals life.

What good does it do to shame someone?

For instance,

If YOU (I am talking to you) see a woman

That is overweight and you are with your friends, are

You going to poke fun at something she is obviously

Struggling with? If you answered yes, I am ASHAMED

!!!

The fact that I am ashamed—disappointed—should be

Taken very seriously.

Happiness is an intrinsic function
That plays hide and seek
With all individuals.

Invisible markings etched
Inside of the unseen soul.
A coding gifted by God
That we, humans, must
Seek to figure out.
(For I cannot read yours
And you cannot read mine.)

No Professor can decipher
The magic to be unlocked
Within an individual's soul—
Their PURPOSE—but they
Will continue to try and fail.

When the wind blows fiercely
Stick out your tongue and let
It pierce it. Can you taste it?

THAT IS LIFE   swimming through
Your taste buds, and ingratiating
Itself as a quintessential aspect
Of your being—because it is.

Sometimes it takes a person,
A book, a movie, a songachurcha-
Dogpetcitystateonandon and on
To "feel" as though their life has been

Fulfilled and he/she is exactly where
They need to be.

I would like to challenge that sentiment.

It appears to me that all of the aformentioned
"things" are simply fillers or distractions. Yes,
they can make an individual experience a tumult
of emotion. However it is covering up the soul's
code embedded in each one of us. To truly uncover
The power you posses, it is necessary to
Look within. Do not look at only the "dirty" parts,
But also seek out the *best* parts and lay it all in
Front of you like a deck of cards. There is a reason
You are here. I don't know it. You don't know it, but
That is part of the journey—figuring it out.
Every single person has done something
He/she regrets whether they are willing
To admit it or not. Be honest with yourself
And others. It is important to set goals for
yourself. It is even more important to FAIL
At hitting the set goal. This will back you into a
Corner and force you to truly analyze why you did not
Achieve your goal and what got in the way. Moreover,
It is important to double-down on how you are
Going to achieve it the second time around.

WHATEVER YOU DO, *DO NOT* GIVE UP.

Honestly, there could be hundreds of rounds until
You finally knock out the beast in your life. (Drug addiction,

Alcoholism, Pornography addiction, Self-Abuse, etc.). The most
Important thing you can do is continually remind the beast it
Does not run *your* life. You don't want to see it anymore, and
Hanging out with whatever you call your beast is, really blows.

Now, I know that each and every person comes from a different
place. So,
Letting go of things, or setting goals, or loving yourself is going
to be more
Or less of a challenge for each person. However, if you are over
the age of
14 and have a brain that allows you to make decisions for
yourself, you can
eventually find the happiness hiding within you. It might take a
24/7 work
week for years, but once you find it, you'll never let it slip away
from you again.
This requires *action*. Everything is at our disposal in life. It is up
to us to seek it out, no matter what it takes. If we truly want
something in life, it is our job to manifest it
Into a reality.

For example,

Charlie wants to write a book, but does not know how. (Charlie
is 25, without a college degree, and works Night Shift at a
Grocery Store).

Q: How can he do this without proper education & such a
mundane life?

A: Easily. With the will to write a book and proper work ethic, Charlie *will* write and publish a book.

First, Charlie reads... which he has always done. However, this time around he does close-readings. Charlie notices the different styles each writer brings to the table. Next, he does not read any yahoo's book! No, he reads Dostoevsky, Tolstoy, Fitzgerald, Hemingway, Pound, Cummings, Woolf, Zadie Smith, etc. This takes time. He reads for years. He takes notes, asks questions, makes arguments against what the writer stated! Charlie is growing confident in his ability to read and write. Charlie is now 28. 3 years of continual learning have passed. Setting goals for himself along the way. Read ten pages a day which turns to fifteen which turns to twenty and so on and so forth. After he peaked his confidence in reading and referencing material, Charlie began to learn the structure of writing. How? He wanted some expert advice so he saved up all the Overtime money he had been getting for the last year to take a class at his county's community college. In the classroom, Charlie gained even more confidence and learned how to navigate his opinion. He also began to network, sharing his goal with his professor (who has published a book and would love to help him!) At the age of 30 Charlie had completed his book and was ready for an editor to help clean it up for publishing. Charlie unfortunately did not know any editors, but he knew it had to be someone he could trust. Over the next year, Charlie met with many different editors and finally found someone he knew would do his dream justice. At 32 years of age, Charlie self-published his book and his dream became a reality. Through trial-and-error, self-discipline, and the want to accomplish his goal, Charlie was able to do what so many of us are not—manifest our dreams. Some naysayers will point out that he did not have many distractions keeping him from success. However, in that seven-year period, Charlie got engaged, his wife had a miscarraige, bought a house, got married, lost his mother, and had two children. The thing he did not do was use any of it as an excuse to not fulfill his personal goal. This journey gave Charlie purpose and reminded him of how challenging reaching a destination can be with all the distractions we experience on a daily basis. Charlie also knew that time would not speed up or slow down for him so he stayed the course and after seven years he arrived.

It is pitiful the way
We use make-up to
Feel more beautiful.

It is disgusting the way
We use hardships
As a scapegoat for failure.

It is terrifying how many
People die without finding
The happiness inside.

Take a look around.
It's a beautiful massacre.

If I cut my finger
I will let it bleed
Until I'm run dry.

The bitter-sweet taste
Of young love,
Torn panty-hose,
And lip-stick.

The shadows will always
Outshine the moon in
The midst of your darkest days.

The sun will always cower
Behind the beaten clouds
When you try to smile.

If I cut my finger
I will NOT wrap it
With a bandage.
I will let it run dry.

There is a path that
I am headed down.
There are two roads—
Millions, really—to travel down.

It does not much matter what road is chosen
Because only the great mysterious GOD above
Knows what is on the path. I'm not god. So, the ignorant
Sheep will get sheared at another's expense.

The toil & blood will keep flowing until there is nothing left.

The dirt will consume our bodies.

The people will speak of our names. (Probably not).

& my finger will bleed until my bones hug my skin—vice versa.

My tongue will hold still behind teeth that once chattered & the voice
That once roused an ear will speak no more.

Horror-stricken minds.

Whimsical humor.

Secular scars.

Prayers with no relation.

I live in the land of the free.

There is always a new problem we are facing.

You are part of the program, but so am I.

We will be until we die.

It is not your decision, and it IS not mine.

So, let us just enjoy this long, TWISTED ride.

There is an infinite posit of hope; it is not rationed. It is not tangible; therefore, it cannot run out. Faith, as well, does not have a finite value. However, there is a correlation between the two. Faith is something one takes from earth; whereas, hope is something that is left behind.

A mindset fixed on
broken things.
A broken mind fixed
on fixing things.

The dead man sings
The live man snores
The two are stuck at
open doors.

The soul's sole purpose
Is to shine.

The dead-live man shatters
while running up heaven's
ladder.

I am in my room holding a broken hanger.

I look in the mirror and see a broken stranger.

Who just tried to kill me with that very same hanger!

I scream with all my rage and anger.

But he keeps coming at me with that twisted broken hanger

I brake the glass and see him scatter across the floor.

The angel on my shoulder tells me to walk out the door,

But the demon shouts louder, "Stay inside to see more."

I pick up all the pieces and puzzle them back together.

I should really go, but it's gloomy, I hate this weather.

The man no longer holds a hanger

His eyes are red! His skin is tough!

He is now filled with anger.

In his hand is a noose?

He tries to put it around my neck.

He says, "this was our truce."

So I step up on the chair and make a knot around the beam...

I take a step and before I know it I can no longer breathe!

I twist and turn with all my might

And suddenly I feel alright.

I snapped the rope from 'round my throat.

I told the demon let me go &

Threw 'way my suicide note.

No matter how hard

it seems to get.

Someone loves you

More than this.

There is always another option.

I want you HERE!

I want you to smile.

I want you to frown,

I want you to do whatever it is

That makes you feel

A-L-I-V-E.

A cow to society MiLK
  ME un-TIL!
I am dry as a July sky.

  HANG ME UP

SIDE   DOWN!!!

shock me and watch me die.

sell me for a profit or toss me
to the side.

breed me for fatality & take away
my pride.

'Cause I am just a cow.

I am food to the flies.

How do you tell someone you love this is it?

There is nothing left for me. I want to give, but I do not have much to give.

I want to love, but no one wants to hold my heart.

I am an anxious wreck. I dwell in sadness. Sadness is my molasses. It is heavy, so I move slowly, but it is sweet, so sometimes I just relish.

I have been blessed with a multitude of life-changing encounters in my life. Times when I changed another persons perspective for the better (I hope), but, also times when another person saved me.

As the years continue to pass, I find myself in a terrible pattern. The years always start and end the same. Trust me, a lot of stuff happens in-between, but yet I find myself in this repetitive cycle.

I do not know why I was put on this earth exactly. To work? To play—but how without work? To motivate? It never adds up. The equation to my life in-particular does not seem to add up.

There are many individuals who have a "talent." Unfortunately, I am not "talented," but I am "good." Good does not cut it. It does not fill that void within each of us. I do not want to keep struggling to find the "one." To work at a "reputable" job. I want to do these things to succeed. However, even if I accomplish all of it, where does it leave me? I will die. You will die. In one-thousand years what percentage of us will matter? All of our efforts will be fairy-tales. It is fake. No one gives a shit about me. Hell, sometimes I could care less about myself. I am sure you feel the same way. It is scary to be alive. There is peace in death. Quiet. When I die, it will be quiet. No friends, no lovers, some family (limited), but most importantly I will be quiet. I often find myself quiet in a room full of people. However, they are very loud, and my mind is even louder. There is always something. I would like it to stop, but it doesn't. This is not a suicide note, although if I was to write one I feel it would resemble this. Am I supposed to thank everyone who "helped" me? Am I supposed to forgive those who wronged me and whom I wronged? It is endless. People change, mostly for the worse from my experience.

If i had to begin again,
Start anew.
The first thing I would do,
Is choose you
and only you.

Sometimes you just need a detox

From all the bullshit

Being shoved down your throat.

Then, and only then, will you realize

You were the one feeding yourself.

I,

Lie naked

On a counter-top

Topped with red

Dresses—some pink.

She loved

Wearing nice dresses.

one for me one for you

one for god above the moon

one for her inside the tomb.

I,

Lie naked with nothing

But a pair of hol[e]y

Socks on that touch the

Bottoms of my knee caps—

on top of smushed (mashed)

lipstick that stained my

one-hundred-percent

Polyester jacket.

one for me one for you

one for god above the moon

one for her inside the tomb.

I,

Want you to lie

With me—naked,

Or not—and watch

The blades on the fan

Attached to the coffee-

Stained ceiling move

Violently without hesitation

Like she used to in the red

Dresses we are using as

Sheets. The quick rhythmic

Motions quelled but she is in

The seashell.

one for me one for you

one for god above the moon

one for her inside the tomb.

Words of the heart

Continuously grapple

    With the words of the mind.

Dying stars sweat

Out life's fever.

Fading in & out

Making me a

Believer.

(In all sorts of things).

A lifeless patient

On a hospital bed.

A thousand scars

With hidden shapes

Like the constellations

Of the stars.

Not another breath

Will that poor soul breathe

She will just wither away

Like when Summer's greens

Fall to Autumn's leaves.

This is solace.

This is peace.

In knowing, she was found

And finally released.

On my deathbed

I will remember

Her solemn features

That sad September.

How she saved me—

A mischievous meddler.

It is frustrating

how poor we are

at amalgamating

how rich You are

at separating. (Good & Evil)?

Honestly,

it is devastating

to wake up to

foggy air fading

and know it is too late

for the resuscitation of

millions of lives

YOU

are situating

chest out & back

straight like a newly

pinned soldier

with high hopes

of escaping

depraved thoughts

of YOUR creating.

There is an inherent dichotomy

In Good and Evil.

We—The Human Race—must

Find the solvent,

Not merely dilute the cacophony

Of left and right leanings.

The abolition of the two-lane street

Is necessary.

One-way streets must be made ubiquitous

In order for us to walk in unison.

Socialism is not the answer.

We must still walk with varying gaits,

And our bodies swathed in a myriad

Of fabric.

However, we must collectively walk

In the same direction.

Perhaps, though, we should run

In order to restore what has been broken

And save ourselves time, for it is surely

Warring us.

If time, and only time, is our only quarrel

Then it seems a calm will sweep across

Us—brothers and sisters—and it will be

Perceivable that we are made from the same dirt.

Our frames, the blood that runs through us, and the tongue

In which we speak, are only a slight difference in our existence.

Although,

I presume we will go on walking backwards, left and right,

Never up, only down, and shouting whatever it is we feel empowered

To shout.

Well, because we are only human.

We leave the true perception of "right" and "wrong"

To the cosmos.

Sometimes it feels like I'm living

inside a confined box with

my thoughts like I have got

schizophrenia

and need some Benzedrine.

I look outside my window and life is but a dream

SO IT SEEMS

but I can see my own reflection when

I look up into the beams.

The light refracts and bends my mind

and honestly 'bout half the time

it feels like I have half a mind

out think just like a mastermind.

With my rhymes I press rewind

and wonder whether I'm divine?

It is so sublime

that I'm confined

inside a room

with all my thoughts

It is like a roller coaster

that always runs and never stops.

Until I hit pause or meet with G(g)od.

Voices start to whisper...

A shadow appears upon the wall...

The curtain slowly opens...

and night begins to fall.

Suddenly,

I DO NOT KNOW

WHERE I AM, AT ALL!

The shadow is getting larger

and I begin to shrink!

The Doctor says "it's just me silly...who did you think?"

She takes a needle and sterilizes the tip. .

[SHE] sticks it in my hip

and everything begins to flip.

I have an eyedea that im nothing but a fish in frozen water.

She asks me if I would like to see my daughter!?

[she] pulls out a notebook so I took [it]

and start flipping through the pages

tons of distorted faces that were faceless.

The doctor closes the curtain

and says, "sorry I have to GO."

the sign above me read

"PLEASE DO NOT ATTEMPT TO LEAVE. THANK YOU!
SINCERELY, THE INSANE ASYLUM TEAM."

I'm just living inside a confined box with my thoughts and I have
got nothing left to do but simply breathe.

\

I have breathed a breath

Of frigid air and thought—

Today is the beginning

Of my *new* life.

Only to find myself

Running backwards to

Where the rabbits dwell.

Suicidal tendencies

could really be the end of me.

Popping pills from Ten to Three

While sipping on some Hennessey.

Or, maybe it is Jack and Coke?

I will smoke until I choke.

Grab the noose & tie the rope!

put my head in and let go.

If I die will you know?

Or, even notice?

All of the feelings

I had

are left on a pad I noted.

Anything I ever said will likely not be quoted,

but being quoted was not the quota.

I look at myself and say I told you.

We all have a place in this world.

Shouting out to you boys and girls!

Do not ever let go.

You will be missed more than you know.

I keep you with me

In my worn, rusty locket.

It is much too old,

One time I lost it.

But, now it sits—Safe—

Inside of my pocket

I pull you out

While I construct

my dreamers rocket.

One day I will blast it

Off to you and no one will stop it.

Around its neck

I will tie my S.O.S, my rusty locket.

I will try

not to cry, but it has been so hard

Since you died.

I know you are high

in the sky

With wings spread wide.

You always told me

angels fly!

So, when my rocket

Passes by

Could you take

A step inside

And come back down?

Go for a ride!

It has been too long,

I miss you Mom.

What did you do this to me?

You twisted my fantasies

And led me to fallacies.

Why are you mad at me?

My life is a tragedy.

Won't you just let me be?

You've put filth in my eyes

Now, it's too hard to see.

Everything's muddy and dark.

You put me down hard.

And pulled out my fragile teeth.

So, now, it's too hard to speak.

Please, will you just let my bones be free?

You do it so casually

Like it's no big deal to see

An imprisoned mind.

A poor, solemn casualty.

Please, Lord shake me from your rotten apple tree.

This is not where I'm supposed to be.

This can't be what's meant for me!

I do not want to vandalize your life.

Or,

see you traumatized by lies.

I still fantasize,

at night

about you by my side.

I'm done seeing through phantom eyes!

I cannot disguise the sickness that is inside my mind

I will be better,

all in time.

I will take it easy,

slow.

You are a flower

that needs light to grow.

I was a cloud

casting a shadow.

I want the best for you in life, truly.

Sleep safe.

Sleep sound.

The good days will come back around.

They always do.

Pull the shade,

So only a crevice

(anything more and i will start to SCREAM)

Of light shines through.

Close the blinds,

(close them, please. i cannot stand the light.)

To block the light

From coming inside.

Shut the door,

On all

Your-hopes-and-dreams

Toss the bandages,

Bleed-and-complain

It is NOT okay.

Call upon the wise,

Pretend it is what you need.

Hey, it is your life...

b-e-l-i-e-v-e what you want to b-e-l-i-e-v-e

Just know I will b-e-l-e-a-v-i-n-g

&

never coming back.

She is an illuminator.
I am an illusionist.
She lignified
my heart
and etched her name.

Days spent together are much too short.
Nights spent away are far too long.

A casualty to society,
a sad song—
is what I once was.
A dulcet voice
which she predicates her love with.

I reciprocate
in a vehement fashion.

I am an uncomfortable kid!
In an UN-comfortable place.

KILLINGMYSELF
At an un-COMFORTABLE pace.

Thoughts flood my mind.
Things (will?) get better.

It all comes in TIME
But-IT-is of the *essence*.

TIME IS NOT REAL

Time IS a treasure
which YOU cannot steal.

The mind is a vessel

that fosters creativity.

It can be a catalyst for change—

new beginnings.

Vile words will infiltrate

the pores

and fill the mind

with toxic thoughts.

Shake them out

and watch them curl

like Autumn's leaves.

Invite love.

Ruminate (bask)

in knowing / understanding

that the heart can

have what it wants

as long as it seeks.

The soul will drift into

unknown territory,

naturally.

Let it move freely.

Do not draw a silver

lining.

A higher being

is navigating its journey.

Feed it positive energy

& do not question its

twists and turns.

It will repay the soul

ten-fold.

The body is a temple

& no two interior designs

are the same.

Treat the temple well

& use it as an example

of how a home should

be treated.

With love, respect, appreciation, and happiness.

PART TWO (II):

SHORT STORIES

Rochester, England: Heaven on Earth

"Why hello there young chap." Is the greeting I imagine to receive as I pass my first bystander, after getting off the plane and arriving in Rochester, England. A multitude of people strolling past on bikes: young and old. I imagine bricks, lots of bricks—specifically burgundy bricks. I imagine a colossal clock tower that is alive; it sits stationary and only speaks when the church bells sound, but it holds a powerful aura over the human beings whom have had the honor of being in its presence. The beauty is striking from corner to corner, yet there is no sunshine to illuminate it, for infinite layers of grey clouds rest in front of the sun. There is a superfluous amount of fashionistas, and a common piece of jewelry dangles above each of their bosoms: a cross. The aroma of coffee lingers in the air, along with stale smoke—from the old fellas' pipes. Around each corner is another coffee shop, residing behind a large glass window. There are dozens of different accents of tea to try, a plethora of coffee-blends, and best of all, a whole wall filled with books: top to bottom! The shelf ranging from the greatest texts of C.S. Lewis to Huxley's classic *A Brave New World*. Time is much different in Rochester, England. The only clocks are read in Roman Numerals, and no one bothers to check because he or she is so caught up in conversation, or reading a book, or taking a nap, that time is the last thing on his or her mind. The medieval looking buildings are draped in the most pure green ivy

in the entire landscape of planet earth—even the chlorophyll is
better there! The atmosphere is lighter, seemingly because the
inhabitants are much less crude. Woman and woman waltz down
one side of the street hand-in-hand as do two males parallel and
the man and woman holding hands in between the two couples
wave to each and wish them a swell day. I imagine waking each
day and slipping into a tweed jacket, corduroy pants, and oxford
style dress shoes; then continuing on to grab a messenger bag
off of my antique-style desk in the corner of my quaint
apartment. The air is always precisely the right temperature,
and the fortunate first breath of fresh air each morning is that
of which has been blessed by the heavens above. Each day to
and fro work, I imagine having a pleasant conversation with the
taxi driver, and there being no honking or cursing at other
drivers. There are libraries instead of bookstores, and ma' and
pa' shops instead of supermarkets. The smiles of one's neighbors
radiate with joy. In any season people swathe their necks with
plaid scarves, and the men leave a faint stubble on their cheeks
at all times. Smoke pours out of factories in various locations
and the train is always moving, but there is no vandalism on the
carts it pulls along the tracks. The denizens of Rochester have a
pedantic nature. It is possible at any moment in time to sit and
have a sophisticated discussion on controversial topics without
one contributor constantly jeering at the other. In the heat of the
summer season—when grey clouds hibernate—the sun pours
over the landscape, snapdragons stand erect in vibrant colors,

and children skip across the cherry mulch to the swing-set, clamoring at one another about who can swing the closest to heaven—I imagine it to be a very religious place. A fine young lady and I get together every Wednesday night at a bench overlooking a river, and observe the stars and correlate the constellations with the happenings in our lives. I imagine the moonlight revealing places in which cannot be seen during the day. There are no savage members of society roaming the streets while the others sleep, causing inexplicable raucous—just the still night. It is easy to fancy oneself to a night out in Rochester; the bars, the stores, the freedom. The closest one can get in finding true peace can be found here, a certain calm occupies one's mind and permeates into the soul, relieving one of unnecessary negativity. Rochester, England is a "Holy Land" where dreams can run wild, friends and acquaintances are aplenty, and love outweighs hate every day. Of course, that is only what I *imagine* it to be like living in Rochester, England.

Medicine Man

"Who are you waiting for?"

"The Medicine Man."

"Who?"

"The Man of Medicine."

"No, what *kind* of Medicine?"

"All."

"He's going to bring you every type of Medicine?"

"That's what they tell me, yes."

"Who's they?"

"Everyone."

"Where does the Medicine Man live?"

"Medicineville."

"That's not real."

"Says you."

"I've never been there."

"Me either."

"Who has been there?"

"They tell me lots of people."

"Who's they?"

"Everyone."

"Is there any documentation of Medicineville?"

"No."

"Then they are lying."

"No. They told me they aren't."

"So, they lied to you twice!"

"Now you're lying."

"How?"

"Because they said they were telling me the truth."

"What's the Medicine Man's real name?"

"He goes by many different names."

"What are they?"

"I'm not going to tell you."

"Why?"

"You don't think He's real."

"Can you blame me?"

"No."

"Then he isn't real."

"Stop lying. Don't you want your Medicine?"

"I don't need Medicine."

"Says you."

"Yes."

"Yes what?"

"Yes, I said that."

"That's too bad."

"What's too bad?"

"That you said you don't need Medicine."

"Why?"

"Everyone needs Medicine."

"Then why don't you just go get it?"

"Now you *sound* crazy."

"Why?"

"You can't get it. You have to wait for the Medicine Man."

"Who is the Medicine Man?"

"I don't know."

"Me either."

"They keep telling me He will come. "

"Who is they?"

"Everyone."

"I didn't tell you that."

"That's too bad."

"Why?"

"You need Medicine."

"Where can I get my Medicine?"

"From the Medicine Man."

"Where is He?"

"In Medicineville."

"Is he actually a Man?"

"That's what they tell me."

"Where did they tell you this?"

"Yesterday."

"Where?"

"I just told you."

"No, you didn't."

"Be quiet."

"Why?"

"I'm talking to the Medicine Man."

"You're talking to me."

"Be quiet."

"Why?"

"The Medicine Man asked me to ask you to please be quiet."

"The Medicine Man isn't real."

"Says you."

"That's true."

"The Medicine Man said you were crazy."

"When?"

"Just now."

"He isn't here."

"Says you."

"What kind of Medicine do you need?"

"His Medicine."

"What is His Medicine?"

"All."

"You're not even sick."

"Says you."

"Is Medicineville on the map?"

"Yes."

"Where?"

"Everywhere."

"How?"

"I don't know. That's what they tell me."

"How long have you been waiting for the Medicine Man?"

"A long time."

"How long?"

"Forever."

"That is a long time."

"How long have *you* been waiting?"

"I don't need Medicine."

"Says you."

"Yes."

"What are you going to do when you need Medicine?"

"Go get some."

"By that time the Medicine Man will be out of Medicine."

"Then I'll go to Medicineville and ask Him for some Medicine."

"Medicineville will be closed by the time you *need* Medicine."

"Why?"

"That's what they tell me. That's why I'm getting my Medicine now."

"Right now?"

"Yes."

"You're still waiting for the Medicine Man to come."

"Says you."

"Is He here right now?"

"No."

"When will He be here?"

"I don't know."

"Okay."

"Okay what?"

"I don't know."

"I feel kind of sick."

"That's too bad."

"Yes."

"I need Medicine."

"Go get some."

"I will wait for the Medicine Man."

"He said it's too late. He ran out of medicine."

"Just now?"

"Yes."

"How?"

"You're sick."

"Says you."

"Yes."

"I really need Medicine."

"I'm sorry."

"When does Medicineville close?"

"It's closed."

"For how long?"

"Forever."

"You were just there, though."

"No, I wasn't."

"Didn't you just talk to the Medicine Man?"

"Yes."

"Tell Him I *need* some Medicine."

"He's all out."

"For how long?"

"To be determined."

"I thought you said forever."

"Says you."

"The sick don't get Medicine."

"Why?"

"That's what they tell me."

"I feel better."

"Good."

"Can I have some Medicine now?"

"Ask the Medicine Man."

"Where is He?"

"Medicineville."

"How do I reach Him?"

"He comes to you."

"When?"

"When He feels like it."

"Who told you that?"

"They did."

"Who's they?"

"Everyone."

"How are you coming along? After the—

"He honest-to-goodness hasn't crossed my mind more than a time or two since then."

Daisy repositioned herself a trifle to the left to flick the ash from the end of her cigarette. Wearing an immaculate black dress Noah had given to her last Christmas, and his preferred shade of lipstick plastered on her lips.

"Well, I'm awfully glad to hear that, honey. It's 1946, the war is over, and there are plenty of men in New York for you to meet. I just wish you would get out of that quaint apartment and have a night to yourself in the city."

Daisy inhaled another substantial drag from her cigarette, and could not cease the upper corner of her left eye from twitching.

"I'm fine mother, no need to *worry* so much. He was a real piece of work anyhow. Can you believe he had the audacity to tell me the only thing I looked halfway decent in is that damned black dress he bought me? He was too much of a want-to-be scholar, if you want to know the truth. He was always juxtaposing the most ridiculous things and using the word goddam at inopportune times, for emphasis in conversation. He was a schmuck, anyhow."

Daisy's finger rapt at an ever-growing pace as the conversation drew on. Her forehead faintly perspired, and her eyes grew thick, lathered with a coat of tears waiting to erupt.

"Well all right, dear. I don't like that use of language Daisy, but barring the circumstances I'll let it pass, this time. If you insist that everything is fine, that's all I want to hear, if you need anything your father and I are just a phone call away. Your father has been worried *sick* about you. I love you, Daisy."

"I love you too mother, tell daddy I said I love him too. Thanks for chatting with me. I think I might leave this place tonight, it's become a tad peculiar."

"All right Daisy, good-bye now."

With that, the dial tone came through the phone proceeding Daisy's mother ending the call. Daisy sat up and did the following: twisted the cap widdershins on her bottle of Kinsley *Gold*, guzzled a significant amount, put on her nicest pair of white gloves, fastened Noah's necklace of Jesus crucified on the cross—which she filched from his nightstand— around her neck, took a step on to the chair positioned in the middle of the room, put her head through the makeshift noose, and hanged herself.

My Dream: 11/11/19.

I was at my dead grandpa's house that is now my alive grandma's house. My mom was there—talking to her dead Dad. I was just listening and not saying anything, really. No one in my family drinks but all their words were slurred & I kept thinking "what?" but was scared if I said something my dead grandpa would leave. I'm 23 and my mom is 24 and my alive grandma is 64 and my dead grandpa is 53 but my alive grandpa (which is impossible) is 62. My 24 year-old mom wanted to show me something in the library so I followed her down the hallway until she opened up the door on her left-hand side. She said, "those are my kids." I am her kid. There was a 4 year-old and a 2 year-old (both boys) which makes sense because I have a 21 year-old brother. Anyway, I was the 4 year-old and I started talking to myself but it wasn't really me because I am 23 and he (meaning me) was only 4. I picked up my brother and he started hitting me softly on the shin—very energetic. I thought to my 23 year-old self that I was very annoying and irritating as a 4 year-old child. I then began to feel awful for my 2 year-old brother who is 21 and has a good relationship with me. All I wanted was love and affection, though. I wasn't trying to annoy anyone. I don't know, the whole thing was sad, really. Very sad.

Shoot. I'm going to be late for my interview.

"Where is my resume, sweetie?" Christ. I can't find my resume anywhere...There it is!

"Never mind, honey. I found it."

Charlotte came sprinting down the stairs, and practically mauled me. Kisses, hugs, kisses. I *really* have to get going. I mean, yes, I love my wife, but Jesus she's got to get off to me so I'm not late. I am sick and tired of living in this little shit hole. I'm a Stanford graduate and finding a *"good"* job in New York is hell. We—Charlotte and I—just found out a baby is on the way. You know what that means? I need to get my shit together and impress the hell out of these suits today.

"Baby, baby. You know I love you, but I really need to get out of here as soon as possible."

She really kills me; those big brown eyes are like quick sand. I can't get caught in quick sand—not today, anyway.

"Alright, baby. Good luck in your interview today. I know they'll love you! Not as much as I do, though." What a girl. Damn, I don't know what I'd do without her.

After about ten minutes, I flagged down a Taxi. Traffic in New York is awful. I'm stuck in the longest damn line of idiots honking like it's a damn language only New Yorkers speak or something. Did I mention New York is hell? I really don't like it here. I'm from Omaha, Nebraska for *Chrissake.* They told me coming here with a Bachelor's from Stanford, I'd surely get a high paying job. Lies. This is my shot, though. I'm only twenty-five, but dammit I really need this job. Finally, the cab driver lets me out at West Street, I glance down at my watch... 7:30 a.m. Perfect, this gives me roughly thirty minutes to get to Bank of America. I feel so damn good, I just start singing. I'm singing at 7:30 in the morning before the biggest interview of my life. Life is good. I don't know what could go wrong, I'm *lucky* to even have this interview to tell you the truth. I had to pull a lot of strings to get an interview here.

"Dad, what's up?" I know my old man loves me and everything, but Christ he didn't have to wake up early to give me a damn pep talk.

"Bren, I don't know how to say this, but your brother Johnny passed away this morning."

This is how it could go wrong. This is exactly how it could become the *worst* day ever. I just talked to Johnny last night. He was going to come over after my interview and celebrate. He had a hankering I was going to get the job. I mean, what the hell do I do? How did he die?

"Bren... You there, Bren?"

"Yeah dad, I'm here. What the hell happened?" My throat was swelling shut, I swear. Suddenly, everything was a blur. My mind would not stop spinning and I was in an irreversible melancholy state. My hands were shaking, tears welling, and I felt like I was going to vomit right outside of my (hopefully) future workplace.

"He had a heart attack, Bren. You know he had drug issues, and I'm assuming it got the best of him this time." His voice was flat as hell. I couldn't tell if he was more upset about my brother's passing or his potential reason for passing.

"I need you to come to the house, Bren. Your mother is going to have a stroke if you're not here. I'm sorry. I will help you get another interview, but you need to be here right now."

All my life, my brother was my hero. He *saved* me so many times. I tried to help him, I really did, he just couldn't break the habit. My brother and I used to be "wild" kids back home. To tell you the truth, I'm the one who introduced him to the shit. Jesus. Why the hell am I so stupid?

"Yeah, dad. I'm going home to pack my things now. I'll be there as soon as possible."

Shit. I have to call Charlotte. She'll understand, I know she'll understand. Johnny did a lot for us. He's the reason I even met her. It's weird, it's like everything I have in my life I owe to him.The last few years have been rough. Dammit. I was looking forward to seeing him today. He was supposed to be on a *plane,* so what the hell? Was he just pulling my leg last night?

"Charlotte, I'm on my way home. My dad just called, Johnny is dead, Charlotte." The words narrowly escaped through the gap in my front teeth.

"Oh my god, Brennen."

"I'll see you soon."

When I was seventeen, Johnny found me passed out in my room, non-respondent. Johnny was only fourteen years old. From what he told me, he picked me up and drove me to the hospital. He didn't know I was suicidal. I was so stupid for doing that, but I was depressed, I was a messed-up kid with a lot of pressure to keep my grades straight, and attend Stanford like dad always wanted. Anyway, he carried me into the hospital and screamed for a doctor, he told me he screamed so loud he might of caused a patient's death that day. When I woke up, I couldn't believe it. I didn't know how I'd gotten there. Mom and dad were at work, and I assumed Johnny was out with his friends. The doctor told me that Johnny saved my life. After that, I straightened up my act and I've been clean ever since. Apparently, after I left Johnny went into a downward spiral. It's tough, though. I was so far away there wasn't much I could do. I tried to phone him, but he never answered. He was pissed that I left him back home. I don't blame him, honestly. We just recently reconnected, and today was the first time I would have seen him sober in years.

When I got back to the house Charlotte was in tears.

"Babe, I'm sorry, but I have to catch the next flight to Nebraska."

I packed my bags, put on my jacket, and kissed Charlotte good-bye. Before I stepped outside, I caught a glimpse of the television screen.

Johnny saved my life.

The summer air was redolent of better days—Days of

Caroline's youth. The steel-blue sky hung over the Watson's

residence, memories of days past rested on the clouds, each one

longing for Caroline to visit.

"Caroline!"

Maggie shouted, giggling uncontrollably as she poked Caroline on
the shoulder.

"Tag. You're it!"

She waltzed away as if she was uncatchable, an innocent

soul drifting through time. Gilded with her shield of innocence.

Caroline watched in admiration, knowing that moments such as

this come and go quickly.

"I'm going to get you, you little stinker!"

Moving at the speed of a tortoise, Caroline scooped Maggie
up in her arms and took her inside.

Three years later Maggie was diagnosed with leukemia,

the doctor sulked into the room and informed Ms. Watson and

Caroline that Maggie had been diagnosed with Acute

Myelogenous Leukemia. Doctor Adams added, "It has spread to

the lungs as well I'm afraid, I'm terribly sorry."—A fancy way

to dodge around one word: death.

That winter, Caroline picked up another part time job on

top of school, to help pay for medical expenses. It took away time for her to enjoy with Maggie. The months dragged on, and that shield of innocence Maggie once carried so blissfully, unscathed, was now tattered and worn. Yet, one night, Caroline arrived home late, after an enduring shift, she noticed Maggie lying on the couch with her head tilted toward the ceiling on the arm rest; the corners of her mouth turned towards the heavens —as if granny was pulling her up there early, and she faintly showed her teeth. Her eyes were half-shut, so Maggie did her best impersonation of the Grinch to not startle her.

"Caroline?" Maggie whispered.

"Yeah, Maggs?"

"Can you sing with me? You know, like old times?"

"Anything you need, Maggie. Anything el--

"No, just sing."

Caroline walked over to Maggie and plopped adjacent to her sister, and gently stroked her fingers across what was left of Maggie's fragile hair. With tears stinging her eyes—worse than a colony of wasps—Maggie began to sing... "I'm sailin' away, my own true love / I'm sailin' away in the morning." The tears seemed to have rolled backwards into Caroline's throat, straining to sing along, she trembled along with Maggie "*Is there something I can send you from across the sea / From the place that I'll be landing?*"

Maggie adored The Lumineers cover of Bob Dylan's *Boots of Spanish Leather*. So they sat, grinning and singing throughout the night. Caroline woke at 1:00 p.m. the next day; but, Maggie did not. Tucked in the small of Maggie's armpit was a Journal, Caroline grabbed it and only one page was written on, it said: "January 17th—last night—was the best night of my life. I love you Caroline to the moon and back. I'm lucky to have a sister like you. Thank you for not getting mad at me. Thank you for loving me, forever."

Tears came faster than the Niagara Falls and Caroline looked down at her sister's face, caressed her cold cheek, and said "No Maggie, Thank you."

Caroline pondered these thoughts as she stood there in awe of the moments that have unraveled to make up her life. Maggie's journal in her hand and the memories in her head, she looked up at the ash falling from the sky like snow. With a final sigh, she turned and walked away, not looking back at what she was leaving behind.

PART THREE (III): SONGS THAT WILL NEVER BE FINISHED.

"Oops, I Got Too High Today."

Chorus:

Oops, I got too high today.
Imma just chill inside my place.
On the couch meditating, namaste.
Thinking 'bout the cookies imma bake.

Verse One (1):

I'm so high i feel like i could fly.
Levitate to outerspace, go for a rIde.
But, I'm stuck inside watching TV in 3-D.
I closed all my curtains, so no one else can see me.
Listening to Jeezy and G with the Eazy.
I can't do Radio Head, it's too creepy.
Eyes getting low, I feel a little sleepy.
I'll leave my phone on incase the homies need to reach me.

Chorus:

Oops, I got too high today.
Imma just chill inside my place.
On the couch meditating, namaste.
Thinking 'bout the cookies imma bake.

Verse Two (2):

Breakin down leaves of grass, Walt Whitman.
Laying on the floor but I'm higher than the ceiling.
This feeling I'm feeling is one in a million.
Just because she celebit doesn't mean she's dealing.
See, I've been having big dreams, they're getting bigger.
And I'm not gonna stop until I'm making seven figures.
But, just to stay mello, I grab the cigarillo, look at my green
friends and say hello!

Chorus:

Oops, I got too high today.
Imma just chill inside my place.
On the couch meditating, namaste.
Thinking 'bout the cookies imma bake.

Verse Three (3):

I don't delegate or segregate,
I separate and celebrate
Then elevate high as heaven's gates.
While people contemplate what's at stake.
You would swear I'm vegan by the way I salivate
when I see them greens up on my plate.
I messed around with luck and fate
which led me straight to destiny.
Sixes penned up on my checks, it ain't nothin but a hex to me.
'Cause when I'm done with this music,
I'm trying to leave a legacy.
Yeah, a Legacy.

Chorus/Outro:

Oops, I got too high today.
Imma just chill inside my place.
On the couch meditating, namaste.
Thinking 'bout the cookies imma bake.

"Dream Journey"

Verse One (1):

The voices and whispers
are coming from demons.
You do not listen...
So, they all start screaming!
But, you're never leaving
'cause it's just a season.
You pull in the air
to know you're still breathing.
Everyone's tweaking,
your thoughts agitated
You're climbing the ladder.
When will you make it?
Sometimes it's too quiet
Panic over patience.
You cannot handle
All their. temptations
But, you're fending them off.
Yeah, you're scratching and scraping
your way to the top
for eternal vacation.

Bridge (Looped Two (2) Times Through):

You lace up your boots
way tighter
than your fingers.
Please take your right hand
off of that trigger.
The problems they only
they only get bigger.
The problems they only
they only get bigger

Verse Two (2):

You've been running
towards the sun and
you are thumbing
through the pages,
Looking at life in its stages.
Always changing,
like the moon in its phases.
Now you're sending praises,
asking for an answer
'cause you've been feeling sick
And you want to rid of cancer.
Forgive yourself in this chapter
to truly live
a hereafter.
The one filled with laughter
and a soul wiped clean.
You must look in the mirror!—
not the TV screen
Because,

Outro:

Life is but a journey, death is just a dream.
Life is but a journey, death is just a dream.
Life is but a journey, death is just a dream.

"This Was Never Titled"

Intro:

Your heart is vacant.
Your mind is empty.
The devil is tempting
you with a rope and some pills,
just to feel an emotion .

Verse One (1):

You're hopeless and trapped
in a field
where nobody's real
everyone lies
and you wanna die
'cause you're sick inside.
You can't hide
the hurt or the sorrow
of not seeing tomorrow.
You rationalize,
while you tie the rope to the beam
in the basement.
Gonna give yourself a facelift.
But save it,
things will fade away.
Don't let it take away your golden days.
If you're trapped in a haze
and you feel dazed and confused
like there's nothing to lose,
then that's just the blues talking.
If you start pill popping,
your problems will pile
and double the trouble will follow
don't swallow the tablets.
The chapter you're living might not be fantastic,
love might be lacking.
Please don't start packing !

You should be laughing.
Everyone wonders how did it happen so all of a sudden?
But never showed love when you needed it most.
They were just ghosts
while you were alone,
but that's how it goes.
That's how it goes

Chorus:

N/A.

Verse Two (2):

Don't let suicidal tendencies
make you another memory,
in a world so cold.
Keep chasing your dreams
hold on to hope
never let go.
'Cause depression will eat
you whole and leave
you on a road filled with pot holes.
It will hope you fall
and don't get up.
If you get stuck,
please look up.
Don't look in a mirror that's broken
and hopeless
distorted and warping perceptions.
Take it as a lesson,
the demons you let in,
pull on your strings just like a puppet.
They love it
when you cannot stomach
ruthless decision
leaving you clueless
and looking foolish.

Dark thoughts start pooling
and you get to losing
grip of the steering wheel.
Nothing feels real
and you can't conceal
these emotions any longer.
But if you're at rock bottom,
you can only get stronger.
Tomorrow are the days
that you long for.
So, hold on, a little longer.
You are the one
I wrote this song for.
Hold on a little longer, a little longer.

Chorus:

N/A.

Verse Three (3):

Back against the wall.
About to lose it all.
Who's gonna catch your fall?
You're sending out lost calls.
You try to clean up,
but the water is muddy.
The scars from the cutting,
all appear bloody.
The voices keep telling
you that you're nothing.
So, you start running
and jumping through hoops.
The noose dangles loose.
You've got nothing to lose,
nothing to prove.
You're stuck in cruise.
Your tank is on E.

You need to believe
and breathe a sigh of relief.
You've been reflecting,
dissecting, digesting
the message you are writing
to try and explain the
evil you're fighting.
Why you've been hiding
inside from all the lies
and all the false idols.
Please don't stay idle!
Movement is vital.
Forgive all your rivals
Erase all the trials you're facing
that keep you complacent
and lockind in the basement
adjacent to dangerous decisions.
There is sinning in living.
So, if you start trippin and
crippling and nobody
is listening.
It can get sickening.
Please don't go missing.
This life is worth living!
Every single day is
a new beginning.

Chorus:

N/A.

Outro:

N/A.

"Chasing Demons"

Chorus:

My hands are shaking.
My heart is racing.
Running from demons
that I think I'm chasing.

I'll come back around,
until they take me down.

My hands are shaking.
My hear is racing.
Running from demons
that I think I'm chasing.

Verse One (1):

I'm paranoid
and I'm stressed out.
I'm a lost cause.
I'm a mess now.
All the people
that I've let down,
they don't need me.
I don't believe
in the problems that pile
it's taking a while
been walking for miles
I can't crack a smile.

Black suit & a black tie!
Running for my damn life.
In my back,
I can feel the knife.
We idolize &
we traumatize ourselves
when we sleep at night

where the demons hide
they can hear us cry
and we wonder
why
we don't feel alive
but don't want to die.

Chorus:

My hands are shaking.
My heart is racing.
Running from demons
that I think I'm chasing.

I'll come back around,
until they take me down.

My hands are shaking.
My hear is racing.
Running from demons
that I think I'm chasing.

THANK YOU

Thank you for reading this. I appreciate each and every one of you more than you know! The creation of this book has been a long road filled with a lot of surprises. I hope you feel better. Anything is possible as long as you stick with it and continually learn and ask questions. Never give up on yourself or those that you love! There is so much to live for... you just have to seek out your passion.

This book is far from perfect, but what is perfect? I want the reader to see the good and bad that comes with the journey. What you write today might be tomorrow's embarrassment. It is all about being comfortable enough with yourself to share it with the world. I hope you loved, hated, or felt indifferent about the writings in this book. That is the beauty of life! It is your decision and no one can make you feel any differently.

NOTES

Lightning Source UK Ltd.
Milton Keynes UK
UKHW021451280220
359515UK00009B/1790